Monster Truck Wars

Jeff Savage

Illustrated with photographs
by David & Beverly Huntoon.

Capstone Press

M I N N E A P O L I S

Printed in the United States of America.

Capstone Press • 2440 Fernbrook Lane • Minneapolis, MN 55447

Editorial Director   John Coughlan
Managing Editor   John Martin
Production Editor   James Stapleton
Copy Editor   Thomas Streissguth

Library of Congress Cataloging-in-Publication Data
Savage, Jeff, 1961--
    Monster truck wars / Jeff Savage
    p. cm. -- (Motorsports)
    Includes bibliographical references and index.
    Summary: Presents a history of monster truck wars which began in 1984, describes the making of a monster truck, explains the shapes and sizes of courses, and concludes with a glossary.
    ISBN 1-56065-258-6
    1. Monster trucks--Juvenile literature. 2. Truck racing--Juvenile literature. [1. Monster trucks. 2. Truck racing. 3. Trucks.] I. Title. II. Series.
    GV1034.S38 1996
    796.7--dc20   95-7180
                                                              CIP
                                                              AC

99 98 97 96 95   6 5 4 3 2 1

Table of Contents

Chapter 1

Monster Truck Wars

Monster trucks are tough. They churn through the mud and soar high into the air. And they crush rows of cars with their monstrous wheels. They are rugged mechanical beasts that destroy everything in their path.

Which monster truck is the mightiest of all? It's the truck that wins the war.

Monster truck wars are competitions. Monster trucks battle to see who reigns supreme. The trucks engage in a struggle for survival. The sole survivor is the champion.

Two monster trucks barrel down the track in head-to-head competition.

Popular Shows

Monster truck wars are very popular. Every year, nearly 20 million people attend these brawls in the United States, Canada, and other countries.

Promoters like USA Motorsports and SRO Motorsports sponsor these battles. The United States Hot Rod Association (USHRA) hosts a series called "Monster Wars," featuring the world's top 14 monster trucks.

Winning

Monster trucks compete on race tracks of various shapes–straight-line tracks, **U-turn tracks**, **oval tracks**, and **round-de-rounds**. All tracks have two things in common–a starting line and a finish line. The winner is the truck that crosses the finish line first.

Race officials call the format for monster wars **single elimination** or the **bracket system**. Only two trucks compete in each heat. The winner of each race advances to the next round. The loser is usually eliminated.

If eight trucks compete in a war, there will be four head-to-head races in the first round. The four winners of those races will advance to the semifinal round. The winners of the two

Bigfoot pops a wheelie at an outdoor event.

head-to-head races in the semifinal round will advance to the final round. The winner of the final round is the champion.

A Second Chance

Sometimes a monster truck can lose a first race and still advance to the next round. This is because each round must have an even number of combatants.

Let's say, for example, that 12 trucks enter the first round of heats. The six winners advance to the second round, creating three head-to-head battles. Those three winners advance to the semifinal round. A fourth truck will be needed to set up two battles in the semifinal round.

How do officials choose the fourth truck? Simple. It is the fastest losing truck from the previous round as recorded by the **Chrondek Timing System**. This system measures the speed of both winning and losing trucks to one-thousandth of a second.

In this way, a truck that loses in the first race can sometimes end up winning the war.

Chapter 2

The History of Monster Truck Wars

Monster truck wars are new. These trucks have not always treated fans to the high-speed thrills of racing wars. Not long ago, monster trucks were slow-moving beasts.

Bigfoot was the first monster truck. Bob Chandler built it in 1974, but it was not until eight years later that the truck became widely known. During the intermission of a truck- and tractor pulling event at the Pontiac Silverdome in Michigan, *Bigfoot* popped out of a tunnel for the first time with Chandler at the wheel. At

Strong suspension allows the tires and truck frames to handle jarring drops to the ground.

first, the crowd did not know what to think of a truck with such massive tires.

Chandler drove *Bigfoot* up to two cars parked in the middle of the track. The crowd watched as Chandler revved the truck's engine. *Bigfoot* pushed into the cars, rolled up on top of them, and crushed them. The crowd went wild. Thousands of people poured onto the field. They surrounded *Bigfoot* and took pictures. The monster truck craze had begun.

The First War

In 1984, 72,000 people filled the Pontiac Silverdome to see the first monster truck war. *Bear Foot, King Kong, Invader, Taurus,* and *Bigfoot* were among the competing trucks.

These monster vehicles took turns driving over a row of junker cars. The crowd roared with delight as the monster trucks crushed the cars. But the event was more of a car-flattening contest than a race. The monsters did not even go a foot (0.3 meter) into the air.

High-Flying Excitement

Seeing monster trucks slowly crawl over **crush cars** was fascinating, but fans wanted more. They wanted to see the trucks go up into the air.

Mechanics worked hard. They developed more powerful engines and sturdier frames to absorb the impact. Soon the trucks were flying high. They began jumping over sets of five cars or more. Next, ramps were built in front of the cars to help the trucks jump even higher.

The high-flying trucks still did not satisfy fans. They wanted to know which trucks could fly highest, turn sharpest, and run fastest. They wanted to know which monster truck was the best of them all.

As often as not, monster trucks are flying through the air.

Tires add one ton each to the weight of a monster truck.

Today's Wars

Promoters created monster truck wars for the fans. Track builders designed courses with steep ramps and sharp turns. To get the best monster trucks in the world to compete in these wars, promoters offered as much as $50,000 in prize money.

The wars were on.

Chapter 3

The Making of a Monster Truck

There are more than 500 monster trucks today. Only the best compete in the wars. Among the best are *Grave Digger, American Gladiator, Snakebite, Awesome Kong, Equalizer, King Krunch, Bigfoot, Carolina Crusher, Bear Foot, UFO, Liquidator, Tropical Thunder, Extreme Overkill, Mongoose, Nitemare,* and *Predator.*

All monster trucks have two things in common–powerful engines and huge tires.

You can see right through the frame of this monster vehicle.

Powerful Engines

Most monster truck engines have custom-built, oversized Ford and Chevy **blocks** with **alcohol-injected blowers**.

A block is the mass of metal that forms the core of the engine. Alcohol-injected fuel does not burn as hot as pure gasoline. A blower (also called a supercharger) pulls more air into the motor. Popular blowers are aluminum models built by the BDS and Littlefield companies.

Most drivers **bore out** their engines. That is, they use a drill to widen the cylinders. Then they add bigger pistons to the cylinders.

Some monster truck engines still use nitrous oxide for fuel. Nitrous oxide is a gas that provides a boost to the engine. A monster truck

Predator leaps off a banked ramp on its way to the finish line. Watch out below!

Weight distribution is important. Getting weigh in the back helps the driver get his front wheels in the air.

engine burns about one gallon (3.8 liters) of fuel for every 100 feet (30.5 meters) the truck travels. Nitrous oxide burns very hot. But it is also very flammable, and is becoming less popular in all motorsports.

Most trucks have their engines in the front. But more and more monster truck drivers are putting their engines in the back to change the weight distribution. *Grave Digger, American Gladiator,* and the new *Bigfoot* trucks now run a rear-engine system.

Huge Tires

Monster truck tires are generally 66 inches (168 centimeters) high and 43 inches (109 centimeters) wide. That is the maximum most competitions will allow. Each tire weighs more than a ton.

Firestone has designed tires especially for monster trucks. After buying these tires, truck owners use a special grinder to cut away more of the tires' tread. This adds traction and reduces the weight of their vehicles.

Frames and Body Designs

Monster trucks fly through the air and crash to the ground. They have to be rugged to absorb the impact. The chassis of a monster truck is the **framing system** on which the body of the truck rests. All monster trucks use steel-tubed frames, because steel is a very sturdy metal. Some trucks use two frames welded together.

Some monster trucks have steel bodies, too. Others have lighter fiberglass bodies. *Grave Digger, Bear Foot,* and *Taurus* are fiberglass-body trucks. American Gladiator has huge and muscular fiberglass arms with clenched fists attached to each side of its body. A fiberglass cobra's head is on the hood of Snakebite.

Suspension Systems

Suspension systems help monster trucks absorb the impact upon landing. The best monsters use **shock absorbers** in a **coil-over** suspension system. In this system, spring wraps around each shock absorber. The spring gives the truck "travel." This allows the truck to bounce more and settle into the ground more softly.

Monsters Are Expensive

Monster truck owners will spend whatever it takes to win the wars. Competition trucks cost at least $80,000 to build. A few cost as much as $200,000.

Almost all monster trucks are about 12 feet (3.6 meters) high and 12 feet (3.6 meters) wide. They weigh at least 10,000 pounds (4,536 kilograms) and sometimes as much as 12,000 pounds (5,443 kilograms).

To win monster truck wars, owners have to build their trucks for bursts of speed. The fastest trucks can go 70 miles (112 kilometers) per hour. They have to be able to glide 100 feet (30.5 meters) through the air and jump to heights of 30 feet (9.1 meters).

And they have to crush cars.

Chapter 4
Preparing for War

To compete in a monster truck war, drivers must register their vehicles. They also must sign waiver forms, which say that the sponsoring organization will not be responsible if the drivers get hurt.

Inspection

Drivers then put their trucks through a **tech session**. In the tech session, a race official inspects the vehicle and its safety equipment. After teching, drivers move their trucks to the staging area.

Monster vans can get into the big-wheel action, too.

Pre-race Conference

All drivers must attend a pre-race conference. At this conference, track officials explain the safety rules.

Qualifying

A competition called **single-lane qualifying** determines which trucks race against each other. Each monster truck makes a timed pass across a set of cars. Usually, officials match the truck recording the fastest time with the truck recording the slowest time. The second-fastest truck will race against the second-slowest truck, and so on.

Wheelie Performances

Sometimes event promoters will use a wheelie performance instead of single-lane qualifying to determine which trucks race against each other. In a wheelie performance, each driver springs the truck's front end into the air and holds it there. The driver then moves the truck forward and backward with its front end still up in the air. When the driver sets the truck back onto the ground, the crowd responds. Officials match up the truck receiving the loudest cheer with the truck getting the quietest response, and so on.

Since officials can measure speed more accurately than crowd noise, they usually don't use wheelie performances to match monster truck opponents.

Chapter 5
The Monster Truck Battlefields

The courses or tracks of monster truck wars come in many shapes and sizes. Some tracks require sharp turning skills. Others demand extra engine strength. All tracks require a little luck.

The Straight-Line Course

The first type of monster truck war course was the straight-line track. On this track, two trucks sit side by side at the starting line. Both drivers watch the starting lights in front of them. When the green light flashes, the trucks take off in a race to the finish line.

Indoor straight-line tracks can be as short as 100 feet (30.5 meters). Outdoor tracks can run as long as 750 feet (229 meters). On straight-line tracks, the trucks must clear a small set of cars or a large set with as many as 14 cars, or maybe both. The key to winning on this track is landing safely after flying over the cars.

The straight-line track is still the most common course used for monster truck wars.

The U-Turn Course

Another course is the U-turn course. This course is shaped like a horseshoe. Again, two trucks race down a straight-line track. But instead of finishing at the end of the track, they make a curved left turn and drive back to the starting line.

Just as in the straight-line course, the U-turn course features jumps over sets of cars.

The Round-de-Round Course

The newest course is called the round-de-round course, also known as the turning course

Tropical Thunder **rolls across a row of junkers.**

or the obstacle course. Two trucks again race side by side. But this time, the trucks make several left turns around the track and finish back at the starting line.

Those big tires can really kick up a lot of dirt. But the crowds love it.

A slower truck can win both a U-turn and a round-de-round course, because the winner is the driver with more driving skills. A powerful engine will not necessarily win on these courses.

The Chicago-Style Course

Some indoor arenas are too small for a side-by-side track. These arenas use a **Chicago-style course** that permits two trucks to compete without racing side by side.

The Chicago-style course is an **oval track**. Each truck starts at a different position on the oval. One truck will start on the upper right portion of the track, while the other truck starts at the lower left portion. The distance each truck must travel to its finish line is the same.

Fans often have difficulty seeing who has won a race on a Chicago-style course.

Chapter 6
Safety

Safety is a major concern for monster truck drivers as well as the promoters who sponsor monster truck competitions.

Safety Precautions

Drivers do everything possible to keep from getting hurt. They wear helmets made of a hard plastic material called **Kevlar**. They wear fireproof suits made of a **flame-retardant cloth**. They wear safety belts across their laps and **shoulder harnesses** across their chests. Every monster truck must have a fire extinguisher in its cab.

The crew rushes to check a monster truck and its driver after a rollover

How important are these safety features? Ask Mike Nickell. He forgot to strap on his seat belt one time while driving *Excaliber*. The truck hit a ramp and soared high in the air. Mike held tightly to the steering wheel. *Excaliber* hit the ground and Mike slammed into the seat. He suffered a broken back. His driving days were over.

The Roll Bar

Every monster truck has to have a **roll bar**. A roll bar is a thick metal pipe placed above and around the driver. The roll bar is solid. With a roll bar, if a monster truck rolls over, its roof will not collapse and the driver will not be crushed.

The Kill Switch

Drivers must also equip their trucks with a **kill switch**. They mount the kill switch on the dashboard and use it to shut down the engine quickly in case of fire.

Safety Crews

A medical crew and a fire crew are at every monster truck war. Two licensed emergency medical technicians (EMTs) stand by with an ambulance. The fire crew consists of four officials who operate the fire extinguishers and fire hoses hooked up to a water truck.

Chapter 7

Monster Truck Competitions in the Future

Car crushing was the most popular monster truck performance of the past. Monster truck wars are popular today. Who knows what monster truck fans, drivers, and race promoters will want to enjoy in the future?

New Trucks

Monster truck owners are always improving their vehicles. They design new suspension systems on computers. The new engines of monster trucks feature the latest in mechanical technology.

New Thrills

Drivers are always looking for new motor-sport thrills. *Taurus* became the first monster truck to crush school buses. *Awesome Kong II* uses a World War II aircraft engine. *Bear Foot* can float.

New Competitions

The Monster Truck Racing Association will probably create new competitions for monster vehicles. These might be monster truck demolition derbies, or races in which dozens of trucks compete at the same time.

For the time being, however, 20 million fans are enjoying the spectacle of monster truck wars.

Glossary

alcohol-injected–an engine that uses alcohol with the regular gasoline fuel

block–the mass of metal that forms the core of the engine

blower–an aluminum device that pulls air into the engine. It is also called a supercharger.

bore out–to make a monster truck engine's cylinders wider by drilling to make room for bigger pistons

bracket system–the format of a monster truck war in which the winner of each race advances to the next round. Also called single elimination.

Chicago-style course–an oval-shaped course that allows two trucks to compete without racing side by side

Chrondek Timing System–a timing system in which a light-operated photo cell triggers a timing box at both the starting and finish lines

coil-over–a suspension system in which each shock absorber is wrapped with a coil spring to give the truck more bounce

crush cars–cars that are lined up in rows to be crushed by monster trucks

flame-retardant cloth–a material specially designed to be non-flammable

framing system–the steel-tubed bars on which the body of a truck rests. It is also called the frame or chassis.

Kevlar–a hard plastic material used to make protective helmets

kill switch–a device mounted on the dashboard that is used to shut off the engine in the case of a fire

nitrous oxide–a gas added to fuel to provide a boost to the engine

oval track–a track shaped like an oval

roll bar–a protective bar (usually a steel pipe) above and around the driver that prevents the truck from collapsing in a rollover

round-de-round track–a track on which competing monster trucks make a series of left turns

shock absorbers–devices on a monster truck that cushion its landing

shoulder harness–a protective belt that extends across a driver's chest from shoulder to lap

single elimination–the format of a monster truck war in which the winner of each race advances to the next round

single-lane qualifying–a pre-race competition in which each monster truck makes a timed pass over a set of cars. Officials use the results to pair up competing monster trucks.

tech session–a pre-race inspection of racing trucks by an official to determine that each truck has certain mechanical and safety features

U-turn track–a track on which competing monster trucks make a single, sweeping left turn

To Learn More

Atkinson, E.J. *Monster Vehicles*. Mankato, MN: Capstone Press, 1991.

Holder, Bill and Harry Dunn. *Monster Wheels*. New York: Sterling Publishing, 1990.

Johnson, Scott. *Monster Truck Racing*. Minneapolis: Capstone Press, 1994.

Johnson, Scott. *The Original Monster Truck: Bigfoot*. Minneapolis: Capstone Press, 1994.

Savage, Jeff. *Demolition Derby*. Minneapolis: Capstone Press, 1995.

————. *Mud Racing*. Minneapolis: Capstone Press, 1995.

————. *Truck and Tractor Pulling*. Minneapolis: Capstone Press, 1995.

Sullivan, George. *Here Come the Monster Trucks*. New York: Cobblehill Books, 1989.

Some Useful Addresses

Monster Truck Racing Association
6311 N Lindbergh
Hazelwood, MO 63042

National Mud Racing Organization (NMRO)
5542 State Rt. 68 South
Urbana, OH 43078

SRO Motorsports
477 E Butterfield Road, Suite 400
Lombard, IL 60148

USA Motorsports
2310 W 75th Street
Prairie Village, KS 66208

United States Hot Rod Association (USHRA)
477 E Butterfield Road, Suite 400
Lombard, IL 60148

Index